BLACK

BRANCHES

For Annie & Bob,
May your' stay
in Montana be a good one.
With admiration
and warm regards,

Greg

6/21/90

missoula

BLACK BRANCHES

GREG PAPE

UNIVERSITY
OF
PITTSBURGH PRESS

Published by the University of Pittsburgh Press, Pittsburgh, Pa., 15260
Feffer and Simons, Inc., London
Manufactured in the United States of America

Library of Congress Cataloging in Publication Data

Pape, Greg, 1947–
  Black branches.

  (Pitt poetry series)
  I. Title. II. Series.
  PS3566.A614B5 1984   811'.54   83-12520
  ISBN 0-8229-3489-2
  ISBN 0-8229-5357-9 (pbk.)

"Black Branches" and "Sharks, Caloosahatchee River" originally appeared in
Antaeus. "In San Antonio," "Put Your Mother on the Ceiling," and "Who Was
Antonio Azul?" were first published in *Black Warrior Review*. "Down the
Road to Canyon Day" is reprinted from *Crazy Horse*. The first section of
"Dolorosa, St. Cecilia, and the Night" was originally published in *The Georgia
Review* under the title "The Night: Ensenada." "On Obregón" first appeared
in *The Iowa Review*. "The Circle of the Year" is reprinted from *Moon Pony
Calendar*. "The Porpoise" appeared originally in *The New Yorker*. "Endless
Nights of Rain" was first published in *Poetry*. "Out Here the Weather" and
"Summer Storm" first appeared in *Poetry Now*. "At the Edge of the River,"
"Part of an Old Story," and "Stanley" are reprinted courtesy of *Quarterly
West*. "A History," "January," "A Job on the Nightshift," and "The Trigger-
fish" were originally published in *Shankpainter*. "Flamingos" is reprinted from
Sonora Review.

The epigraph on page 27 is taken from "Love Poem," by William Carlos
Williams, *Collected Earlier Poems*, © 1938 by New Directions Publishing
Corporation. Reprinted with the permission of New Directions Publishing
Corporation.

My thanks to the National Endowment for the Arts for a fellowship in poetry.

My deepest thanks to Linda Fry, Lance Patigian, Garrett Kaoru Hongo, Allen
Wier, Dara Wier, and Marnie Prange for their friendship and encouragement.

*The publication of this book is supported by grants
from the National Endowment for the Arts
in Washington, D.C., a Federal agency,
and the Pennsylvania Council on the Arts.*

for Marnie
and in memory of Colie

CONTENTS

I.

The Triggerfish 3
Flamingos 5
Stanley 7
Bailar 8
At the Edge of the River 10
The God Box 11
The Yes and the No, Redondo 14
Put Your Mother on the Ceiling 17
Delvin's Dream 19
Summer Storm 20
The Circus Elephants 22
Sharks, Caloosahatchee River 24

II.

In the City of Bogotá 29
A Job on the Nightshift 31
For Beroë 33
On Obregón 35
Endless Nights of Rain 36
Black Branches 38

III.

Part of an Old Story 45
In San Antonio 48
Out Here the Weather 50
Winter Night Under Black Mountain 52
January 54
A History 55
Down the Road to Canyon Day 57
Horses on the Highway 59

CONTENTS

IV.

The Circle of the Year   63
The Porpoise   64
The Night: Gulf Shores   66
To Sleep   68
This House   70
Dolorosa, St. Cecilia, and the Night   72
Who Was Antonio Azul?   80

I

THE TRIGGERFISH

Leaves of mangroves rattle
in the breeze. A gray rowboat
knocks against pilings at the end

of the dock, and the years
hold still around this moment.
Boat, water, and sky

are all the same color.
A boy kneels on the whitewashed boards
of the dock and stares

at the dull gray water, waiting.
Waiting for something beautiful
or monstrous to come up to him

from below. He has heard the stories
of devilfish, seen the silver tarpon
tailwalk on the water in moonlight.

He is patient, a watcher
held in a physics
he is yet to understand.

Above him a great ledge of cloud
moves in from the Gulf
hauling thunder and a slanting

curtain of gray rain.
Below are the clouded rooms
of redfish, snook, shark, and manatee.

He is beginning to live
in those rooms above and below
opening within him.

And as the brilliant slow-finned
triggerfish drifts up
out of the gray water

of the sound and mouths
a circle on the under surface
of water

a fish of equal color
rises in the boy
and goes down to meet the other.

FLAMINGOS

I imagine them now
as they are sometimes seen
in great flocks flying over the Andes,
a sacred movement of birds and light.
On Sundays like this
I have glided around that point
of shaggy mangroves
off the west coast of Florida
in a canoe as the sun
slipped into the Gulf
and spread out its silks
on the water behind me,
a small boy astonished
at the world and his own mind
a few big hushed moments
in a bad year, 1956.

I like to say
I was born in 1947
just outside the city of Eureka, California
because it's true and has
a good sound. I was born
again to the strange loveliness
of this earth on that Sunday
gliding on the waters
of Pine Island Sound
around the point
through the secret opening in the mangroves
into Addison's lagoon.
My stepfather in the bow
held his finger to his lips
then pointed toward the far shore.

I held my breath and listened.
At first I didn't see them
just a rose glow on the water,
some part of the sunset broken off
and left behind.
But as we drifted quietly closer
I was filled with a single word,
Flamingos . . .
though I was wrong
and was told, in a whisper, Spoonbills.

Now I see them
preening, dipping their odd bills
into the water, swaying
in a kind of unison
on long thin legs.
Startled at the wrong word
they stiffen, bow to the water
and lift in a great shock of pink feathers
flaming into the air.
And I trail after them
all my senses stunned by the power
of a word as they fly away
toward the west
growing small and dark
on the evening sky.

STANLEY

He was a big man,
I used to hang on his arm.
He called our mother Ramona

though her name was Irene.
He worked hard, sweated a lot.
He wore khaki pants and T-shirts

could drive a nail with one blow
didn't smoke didn't drink.
But once in the evening

he knelt on the floor
before the big stuffed chair
covered with burgundy roses:

give it another try, he said
and he laid his head
in her lap and cried.

Where do the failed fathers go
after the jobs are lost
and the money runs out

and tears have dried to salt?
They turn to snow?
They drive blue Fords to Mexico?

We know what the mothers do,
they take us with them
wherever they go.

BAILAR

I remember dark lounges
and smokey honky-tonks
I visited with my mother,
who found friendship, and solace,
and trouble there.
I listened to the talk as I listened
to the waves, the hush and applause
of sand and surf. But the music
was my own heartbeat
and I danced
in front of the jukebox
for joy
and the amusement of the drinkers
who flipped quarters at my feet.

Later I learned the hunched gait
of indifference. Hands in pockets,
inward turned shoulders, the boy's body
holding in desire, ready for blows.
A new language.
The dancing I did
was in a darkened room beneath the gymnasium.
We practised the shuffle, the slow stride,
all the postures of the blues to come.
We moved to the Deltones, the Drifters, the Miracles
into friendship, solace and trouble.

Then once in a bar in Mexico
I got drunk on tequila and danced
all evening, alone in another language,
in front of the jukebox.
And because I was drunk
I stared, with my head down,
at my shoes to make sure
they touched the floor.
The men at the bar
kept shouting *"¡Levanta la cabeza,*
Levanta la cabeza!"
I didn't understand
what they were saying until one man
got down from his bar stool
and began dancing, with his head
held high, demonstrating for me
the proper way for a man to dance.

AT THE EDGE OF THE RIVER

Sometimes you must forget everything
then remember it all: the grass, the seclusion
of buckbrush, the small fire you built
in the rain, enough to warm
your hands, and the barking
of the black collie as he raced away
over the wet field on the trail of a doe.
In one corner of the field
wild asparagus grew, at the other
a path led away, turned twice in the oaks,
passed a scarred sycamore, parted
the brush and gave out
at the edge of the river.
You closed your eyes and listened
to the hissing of rain on the river.
It sounded like fire.
Forget the man with the small brass plate
fastened by wire to his throat
and the hole he had to cover
with his finger when he spoke.
Forget him as you've forgotten
what he said that frightened you.
It was not the words but the whistling
sound they made. He was not your father
or your future, but only the man
standing next to you in the rain
when you opened your eyes.

THE GOD BOX

Near the end
Ada's heaven was the inside
of a certain mountain in Colorado
where the followers of Saint Germain
gathered to learn the business
of the angels.
It must have been awkward
there in the presence of the everlasting
learning the grace that such living
would require for a small woman
born in Isham, Tennessee
among the secret trees
and coalfields of Appalachia.
Or maybe it was easy
after the hard work
of living in this world
where she gave birth to nine children
and raised eight, where coal dust
and the smoke of memory slowly
turned her husband's lungs
to stone.

Her way to cure a fever
was to sweat it out.
And we believed her
when she told us she knew
what was wrong with us.
She proved herself again and again
as she cleaned and washed
and whistled, through her teeth, the old
sad hymns.
She believed in the old ways.

She was willing to try the new.
There was no suffering
that could not be overcome
she believed.

When the salesman came to the door
of her last hard-earned home
in the city of angels
and told her they had invented
a machine that could put you
in direct touch with God
she must have believed him.
She paid over four hundred dollars
for it. It was the time
of the first television sets
and it was hard to question
the miracles of technology.
The miracles of God
were beyond question.

In the back bedroom of the house
on Juanita Street the afternoon sun
burned through the blue gingham curtains
the day she set up
the God box
and plugged it in.
Jim and I sweated and wheezed.
His cancer and my asthma
wiped out the years
and we were more like brothers
in our misery
no longer separated by two generations

and Ada was our stern angel
holding the cool cloth
to our foreheads, holding off
all that would come to claim us.

She took blood from our fingers
with a sewing needle
and pressed it on a square
of blue paper and fed
the paper into a slot
on the face of the black box
that would save us.
It looked like the instrument panel
of a warplane
with its dials and lights.
We watched as she sat down
before it and bowed her head
and prayed and held tight
the serious black hand grips.
We watched a long time.
When the machine sparked blue
and Ada began to shake
and hum and the machine
vibrated and the lights flashed red
something changed in us
if only for one good moment
when we knew she would do
anything for us and we believed
she believed and we felt
the presence of Ada's God
alive and electric
racing through the room.

THE YES AND THE NO, REDONDO

Look west and there's the sun
going down to sit
on the pan of the Pacific.
Look east and there's the haze
of freeways, the crown of industry,
the amber blanket of bad air
over the city that can't sleep
for dreams and the need
to dream. Straight up
the sky is still blue.
There's a small constellation
of daystars flashing, jets
in formation for a routine
pass over the Channel Islands
.where the sea birds whiten
the rocks and the seals grovel.
To the pilots all this
is beautiful and abstract.
They can't smell it.
Look down, as a child would,
into the water where perch
are nudging barnacles on the pilings.
They swim in and out of sight
at ease in their silent bodies.
Perch are hard to hook, but kids
catch them and fishermen use them
for cut-bait. The gulls clean up.
The gulls glide around us
like the hours, or rock on the water,
small arks of attention
among fishing lines and floating debris.

The *City of Redondo*
with its load of fishermen
is rumbling out toward
the big mouth of South Bay.
But it's not the fishermen
I want you to see. It's that
boy standing on the roof
of the bait shack above
the sign that says, "No diving
from the pier." He looks
at the man standing below him.
Talk me down if you can,
he thinks, go ahead, try.
Then he looks out over the Pacific.
The waves wash up the beach,
steel brushes on a snare
tuned tight. He'll fly
through the air, he'll see his baby
tonight, rock 'n roll
in the surf of her
till he's out of breath. That's her
over there at the railing, calling,
fly boy, do a trick,
I'll keep you warm, take you home
give you something good
that you don't got.
You can't hear that
because she's talking with her eyes.
So go ahead, he thinks, call the cops.
Pull me down. Go ahead, try.

Today's the day he finds out
about his own yes and his own no.
Desire and distance fill him
as he leaps into the air,
frightening the gulls.
She loves the way he keeps
his arms spread his chest out
as he falls, against the law, forty feet
into the green waters of South Bay.
The way he enters the water
like a slick knife
with hardly a splash.
And she tells him so
as she greets him now
in the shadows among the pilings
under the municipal pier.
And later she will do her best
to keep all the promises
that shine in her eyes.

PUT YOUR MOTHER ON THE CEILING

In the schools of Arizona
we used to play a game
put your mother on the ceiling.

What is she wearing?
What does she have in her hands?
Is she happy or sad, or can you tell?
If she is speaking, what is she saying?
Is she looking at you or looking away?

Some days the walls backed off,
the ceiling lifted, and there were
many women, real women
over our heads held up
by the light in our eyes.
They wore long turquoise dresses,
bright sweaters, beads
and concho belts, T-shirts
that said Kiss, Phoenix Suns, Ford.
They held babies, knives, baskets,
cans of beer. They were laughing
or weeping or watching TV.
They said shut up, be good, I love you
in English, Spanish, Navajo, Apache, and Pima.

Now and then
one of the women whose name
might have been Nina Pancho, Charlotte
Keesay, or Josie Allison,
one of the mothers
who wore a white dress

and perhaps a hat of live
hummingbirds and held in her hands
wild flowers and dollar bills
looked down on all of us
smiling, saying "Come home, come home."

On other days some of the mothers
failed to appear. They were hidden
among other concerns.
A girl by the window might say,
"I can't put my mother on the ceiling,
my mother is dead."
Then she would look out
over the schoolyard toward the motherless mountains
and the ones who were there above us
would close their eyes, go mute
in mid-sentence, and fall
embarrassingly in the aisles,
all of them having died a little
in the finality of the words of the girl.

DELVIN'S DREAM

Delvin Catha had a dream.
He was traveling on a train
with his mother.
He didn't know where he was going.
He was cold, so he left his seat
to look for the cardboard box
in which his mother
had packed his clothes.
He wanted to put on his sweater,
but when he found the box
and opened it
there was a dead man inside
wearing a black suit and black shoes.

Delvin returned
to sit with his mother.
When she asked him where his sweater was
he told her he couldn't find it.

He didn't tell her
that even his small life
had become difficult,
that the night, if only for an instant,
had dressed him in the black suit
and shoes of the dead.
Nor did he complain of the cold
or question the journey
but sat down like a good child
beside his mother in the dream.

SUMMER STORM

A boy was playing
on the municipal golf course
when the storm began.
He ran to the shelter
of a cottonwood to escape the rain.
Lightning struck
and the tree exploded.
Witnesses told how the boy's heart
refused to beat, how on his chest
was burned the outline
of a St. Christopher medal
he had worn for luck.
Later people gathered
at the Grant Road bridge
to watch the river come to life
after a hard rain.
They parked their cars
and strolled out to see
what the river would bring:
fence posts, feathers, the hood
of a car stalled at a crossing
near Tumacacori, a disheveled rooster
perched on the bloated body
of a steer.
A woman in a red dress
crossed herself and wondered aloud
where the river was going.
The man beside her
shook his head and frowned.
When no one was looking
a boy leaned over the railing

and dropped a beer bottle,
then ran to the other side
to see it shine, an amber jewel
as the sun touched it
for an instant
before it sank in the muddy water.

THE CIRCUS ELEPHANTS

Bulls they call the circus
elephants, female or male.
Lot Lice they call us.
We come early to watch
the elephants rock
against their chains
lean their enormous heads
against the consoling shoulders
of their brothers and sisters.

Their trunks sway
like ropes of ships
lost in the sea.
Their eyes like agates
set in boulders
look steadily on the crowds,
the green-haired clown
hawking *bibles,* children
carrying candy like torches,
the blind faces of trucks
the calm faces of horses.

When the show begins
the elephants rear up
on their hind legs,
curl their trunks
like question marks
in the air and children
suck in their breath
as though they are
falling into deep water.

The elephants, composed
as the dream that holds
the tent up.
They'll do almost anything
for us. They'll dance,
they'll bow, they'll poise
their huge weight
over the body of a woman.
And one, if you watch closely,
will always whisper
in the ear of the tiger.
Can you hear me sweetheart
we're in this together.

SHARKS, CALOOSAHATCHEE RIVER

It is so quiet. It is 1957.
You can place the year
by the fins of the new cars
lined up in the parking lot of the Gulf Motel.
Even in the middle of the day
the rooms are dark, rooms
where lovers thump their beds
against the walls, where someone
goes to sleep forever with the radio playing.
You can't hear the river in those rooms
although the river never stops.
It goes on flowing gray to silver
down through the glades and forests
where the people lived who named it
Caloosahatchee.

A boy opens a door and steps out
into the shock of sunlight, the flashing
chrome of bumpers and grills.
In the shadows between the cars
sparrows peck at the asphalt.
He watches as men line up on the dock
the bloody sharks they caught.
The fins gleam like the waxed fins
of the new cars. Their eyes don't close either.
After the snapshots and jokes
they heave the bodies back into the river
and stroll off to their separate rooms.

They say a dead shark
sinks so slowly its body
is dissolved by saltwater
before it reaches the bottom of the sea.

There in the Caloosahatchee, in the shadows
between the long bodies of sharks
the current pulls toward the Gulf.

Then it is Sunday. The boy's mother
still sleeping, he leaves the darkness
of the room with a quarter in his pocket
and walks a few hundred yards of sunlight
along the river to the Arcade Theater.
It's cool and dark, just a few kids waiting
for the matinee. The screen,
blank silver like the river. Dreaming
and quiet, he could be anyone. He is
the little brother of sharks, a boy
who slips into a car and guns the engine.
Tires burn, blue smoke shoots up, fins
slice the sunlight. Blank eyes and grill
grinning the car speeds across the parking lot
off the dock and into the river.
It sinks so fast, the river so shallow
you can hear the thud of rubber
on the bottom before white water calms
and it's gone.
The doors to the motel open
one by one, light streams in, people walk out
and gather as the boy steps dripping
from the river. No one speaks a word
but stares, as he does, at the water.
The only sound is the murmur of the river
as it moves toward the Gulf. They will listen
until they hear.

Or, more likely, the boy is knocked unconscious
and never steps from the river. The sheriff's

boats drag the bottom with nets and hooks.
Divers search for the body in the gray murk.
But he is gone, drifting with sharks, gone
in the silver glinting on the river.

II

*Who shall hear of us
in the time to come?
Let him say there was
a burst of fragrance
from black branches.*

—William Carlos Williams

IN THE CITY OF BOGOTÁ

The statue of a rich industrialist
stands in a small plaza
in the city of Bogotá.
People wait in line to whisper
their prayers in his bronze ear.
Pigeons and the leaves shadow them.
A *gamin*, one of the boys
of the streets, is asking for coins,
cigarettes, but receives instead
a small blessing, a hand
on the head and the sign of the cross.
Rain that was falling moments ago
glistens on the slick black hair
of the soldier at the curb
and on the barrel of his rifle.
Water beads are caught in the blue
wool of a woman's sweater, a woman
who looks at her shoes and waits.
A girl stares over the tops
of the buildings and listens still
to the rain moving away
over tin roofs toward the mountains,
a sound like the applause
of a distant multitude.
There must be girls all over
the world listening into the distance
like that. I don't know
what the soldier is thinking.
But I know the fatherless
wild boys of the streets.

And I know there must be
someone who will listen
without judgment to the secrets
and prayers that grow in us each day.
Water drips from the bronze ear
as the woman takes her turn there,
her hands hidden in the sleeves
of her sweater. As she whispers
the pigeons fly, funneling up
into the air above the city of Bogotá
to celebrate the end of rain,
each one a word resisting
everything that conspires to silence.

A JOB ON THE NIGHT SHIFT

He is the prince of tin cans
here on the nightshift.
His job is to pick up
what has fallen, to crawl
among the constant gears
beneath the conveyors
that carry the regiments
of cans, the peaches
jostling under the gloved hands
of women who joke or curse
in Spanish under the nightlong
surging of engines.
He stops and leans
on his dolly to stare
at the fluent hands of the women
as they sort the fruit.
So many peaches the hands
fly over, so many nights,
so many voices hushed
or lost, so many peaches,
so many nights, nights
that carry him south
on the road to Magdalena
where the shadows hunched
over fires in oil drums
are dead men, uncles, brothers.
And the children run
in the night streets,
coils of firecrackers
snapping at their heels.
He can almost see their faces
but the foreman touches
his shoulder and orders "move it."

So he moves it
loaded with fallen cans
out the back door of the cannery
to his station under the stars
and yellow bug lights.
His job is to salvage
what he can. He has
a tool for straightening them
and a tank of cool still water
to wash them in, a tank
of water where the yellow lights
float among the power lines
and the stars, and when he bends
to his work over the water
there is the prince of tin cans.

FOR BEROË

When the rising waters
of the gulf
enter the river Chao Phraya
the current slows
and brown silt clouds the surface
as though pushed
by great fins.
A girl stands on a dock
with the river beneath her
watching the traffic of small boats,
how they bob in the wakes
of larger boats.
If she smiles
or laughs like the lost
what is it that moves her
as she watches the river?
It's not the reflection of the sky
or a passing boat.
It's not the golden slipper
of the queen of Thailand
drifting out to sea.
Maybe it's something she sees in the water,
a light that comes from beneath.
When the tide goes out
she is till there watching.
The water has slid away
beneath her. Black mud
steams in the sun
marked by the river's flow
littered with the garbage of the people
and smelling of oil.

She holds her breath and waits
for the tightening inside.
If she cries sometimes
it is for no reason she can name
but the tears that stain her cheeks
are muddy like the river
as though the river
had gotten inside her.

ON OBREGÓN

Across the street
from the only cottonwood tree
on the Avenida Obregón
there is a white burro
harnessed to a cart
that has stood still
for over a decade.
Between the long white ears,
a gaudy paper flower.
Beneath the slung belly, between
the four patient legs, a bucket
that now and then a man
empties in the gutter.

All day, the flashing
of gold watches, the thin rustle
of money, like the flower
between the burro's ears, the traffic
in baskets and plaster saints
the blaring staccato of trumpets
the thumping of the guitarrón,
all the jive and sorrow
of two or three languages.
All day the tourists eat and pay.

Children laugh
and slap the burro's flanks.
Flies ride the flicking ridges
of his ears. It's all the same.
The sun moves slow on the burro's back
as he stares through the exhaust
of failing trucks at the great cottonwood
with which he shares, in his way,
the dignity of a rooted life.

ENDLESS NIGHTS OF RAIN

Did you have relatives
among the dead? the man
in the black felt hat is asked.
His dark poncho hanging like a shroud
over his clasped hands, he stands
in the little cemetery
on the edge of the village of San Mateo Ixtatán.
Around him the green walls
of the mountains and the conspiring shadows
that circle his world like bad weather
won't let him answer.
On the other side of his gaze
under his hat the leaves
are bloated with rain and he
is a man waking again
to the sound of gun fire
and the cries of his neighbors.
Relatives among the dead?
He does not answer. He no longer
trusts the simple truth.
It is 65 kilometers to Huehuetenango.
Where he stands it is 36 lives
away from the first of June
and all the living and the dead
are relatives where he stands.
Rain drips from his black hat
and a small shadow covers his eyes
where a whole country is hiding.

§

No one seems to know
who they were: the army
of the rich, the army of the poor,
the army of the rich
dressed in the clothes of the army of the poor.
No one knows whose souls
are tangled in the trees and vines
in the darkness of the mountains
outside the towns
or why the soldiers came
to kick in the doors of the sleepers
and gather the players and deal the hands
in the game called endless nights
of rain. For blood or money,
no one's sure. But the soldiers,
trained in forgetfulness, must have agreed
that their mothers were whores
that their own bodies were weapons
with which to stab out the lights.
And it goes on every night,
the rain and the killing
in some foreign country of the heart.

BLACK BRANCHES

for W. Eugene Smith

Nine years ago
I studied the photograph
of the shrunken corpse
of the soldier of Iwo Jima
and understood the meaning of war,
which is to say I understood nothing
but saw the black branch
in the burnt sleeve,
and under thin leather
of a once human face
shadows of all the rivers
turning to dust.

§

Outside my window
the curve-billed thrasher
perched on one leg in the Palo Verde tree
fluffs his feathers
to keep off the cold.
One leg stiff and useless,
somehow maimed, sticks out of the feathers
like a small black branch.
This fierce-eyed bird wavers
and nearly falls from the tree
but hangs on
with one good leg
and sings against the cold.
I will give him seed
to help him through the winter.
I will name him Gene Smith
in honor of one who died.
In honor of the watcher

at the window
who looked down
on the flower district of Sixth Avenue
and saw men and women
carrying their lives along
in bundles and bouquets and paper bags
through whatever weather the streets held
through slick rain and snowdrifts
through the smells of exhaust
and flowers with their umbrellas
and their overcoats and their canes.
Who watched them slip into taxis
or patrol cars or some barely
visible pockets of despair
drifting the city streets.
Who saw them stop
beneath his window
to argue or embrace.
Who found in the instant of seeing
something he wanted to take from them
some gesture to fix and give back
some curve of shoulder under the weather
or careful crook in the arm
or shadow defining.

§

Juanita looks past
the first leaf.
The twigs are beginning
to pulse again.
Darkness surrounds her;
the centers of her eyes
are made of it.

39

And light floats there
in the eyes of the nun
waiting for survivors
or news of death
after the sinking of the Andrea Doria.
Either way she, who has given
her heart to an effigy, who knows
in her own spirit the dark
presences and the light,
holds her human fingers to her lips
and waits, her still hand
more lovely than the glitter
of sunlight on a calm sea.

The hands of Professor Jones
of Piney Woods hold each other,
sure and calm, his fingers
like so many brothers and sisters
sleeping on a bed of bone.
And he turns his face up
like one more leaf to the light
and would root there and grow down
were it not for one shy thumb
hooked in the lapel
like an anchor in the human world.

Nine years ago
I turned the page quietly
and looked down on the head
of Albert Schweitzer and admired
the intelligent silver arcs of his hair.

His hands weren't in the picture
but I recognized the attitude of a man,
a little uncomfortable, shuffling his feet
and looking down at his dusty shoes.

That's how Smith saw him:
bent down into work or thought,
"one man laboring to accomplish
according to his beliefs."

But he also saw the Nubian goats
standing on the corrugated tin roof
of the leper's shed
looking down on the village,
and perhaps later in the darkroom
heard their steps above him
and the sound of the rain
and the laboring breath
in the dark beside him.

§

Now I live with his ghost
and his photographs. I sleep
in his bed, or don't sleep.
I feel the shape of his
abused body in the mattress
and below that a dark well
dug by a squatter, abandoned
and reclaimed by some creature
who built in it
a nest of black branches.

He's still alive down there
in that secret darkness.
That dark that *Life*
wanted to remove from his photographs.
The same dark that bent over
the village of Deleitosa in Estremadura
and shaded the eyes of the Guardia Civil
and sucked out the eyes of the Abuelo
and sounded in the belfry and hooded
the women. The dark pressed open
by a thousand shoes
on snowy sidewalks of the Avenue.
Dark that clamped down
on the mad ones of Haiti
that burned under the bandages
and listened in the Cathedral,
that slept in the velvet of the cello case
in the feathers of the egret
in the warm waters of Minamata.
That ate its way into the bricks
and into the lungs of Pittsburgh.
That stood at the window
with the miniature animals and the dolls
and looked out on the new day.

III

PART OF AN OLD STORY

1

Driving north through the hills
above the Colorado River
I didn't know that I
was part of an old story:
nightfall in a strange town,
the tired traveler
revived by the song
of a beautiful woman.
I didn't know, as the radio
helped me over the miles,
that a white mustang
was making his way
down the rocky hillsides
toward the scent of the river.
If you had told me
that in a floating casino
I'd watch a blind man
leaning an ear over a crap table,
rolling dice and unrolling hundreds,
I'd have laughed.
But I was part of an old sadness.
I couldn't remember what
I did know, only this landscape
of rock and shadow
cooling toward night.

A lone coyote carried
the last fire of twilight
in its fur for a moment
then disappeared in the rocks.

Hawks and doves along the highway
were the same black
perched on wires or
flying the last light.
For miles I imagined the color
and elegance of feathers
while night went on borrowing
the distinctions of the living.
Maybe these things are passed on
at random in human dreams.
I didn't know.
Then the road curved
and dropped toward the river
and a narrow strip of rich bottomland,
the alfalfa fields of the Mohave.

2

If I were the horse
that reared up in the path
of the tired traveler
and turned to a sudden statue
of light
the blind gambler
would throw down the dice
and the old sadness.
If I were the river
I would've stopped for one white instant
in the brain of the horse
and then gone on past
the strange town, quietly
holding up the floor of the casino.
If I were the sheriff,
a more or less honest working man,

who put a bullet
through the horse's rivered brain
to be sure,
I would know
I was part of an old story
that is often complicated
by beautiful women and strangers.

3

There was a silence
that even the river acknowledged
as the sheriff held his handgun
over the horse's temple.
When the shot was fired
the horse's white legs stiffened
as though they leapt from the earth.
The body rocked
in the wet weeds,
a shudder rushed over the flanks
and it was still.
The sheriff lit a cigarette
and leaned on the open door
of the patrol car
and watched the glow
of two taillights recede into one.

IN SAN ANTONIO

for Richard Hugo

We flew in over the Devil's Backbone,
Balcones Escarpment, the dark Texas hill country
to the north where caliche roads branch
white in moonlight and landed at four
in the morning in sleeping San Antonio
an hour before the roosters of Spring Branch,
Blanco, and Johnson City began crowing
the harsh six-note at the sun.

In the cab on the way into town
I sat in the front seat with the silent driver
watching the new amber lamps that light
the Interstate. I remembered crossing the country
in the cars and trucks of strangers,
passing a bottle of blackberry brandy
back and forth with a man
who put his hand on my knee
and sang "T for Texas T for Tennessee"
and I said let me out here
when he might have taken me to Houston or further.

Out here
God and the Devil's Backbone
are made of the same rock
that rises above the grass and live oak.
And there's a road that runs
along that ridge where I sat on a suitcase
in the back seat of a '52 Buick
so I could look out the windows
for the hawks and the horses and the city of San Antonio.

I was in love with my mother
and still remember how she said it
like a gift, "the Alamo, we're gonna go to the Alamo."
I didn't know then what I know now.
In San Antonio the ghost white stone of the Alamo.
I didn't know how we tend to get lost
in each other's cities
where all that is given or broken
by the days passes through us
like a river that outruns its name.
In San Antonio the river is green and tame.

OUT HERE THE WEATHER

On the pier a child
lost his cap in the wind
and stood there watching it
float away in the water
untouchable as the future.
And a woman walking in the same wind
squinted through tangles of blond hair,
her patchwork skirts lifting,
something inaudible held close
to her lips. In the darkened
window of a storefront
a fisherman in a flapping raincoat
read in his own face
the long months of uncertainty.

Out here the weather
works its salt into the heart,
darkens all the faces
then lights them up.
Gulls idle in the wind.
They stand on one leg
and ignore each other's cries
for hours, they float
all night on the black water
then lift themselves effortlessly
into the air.
We are not like them.

Out here the weather
can make a wilderness of the streets
or fall on you like a father's hand
heavy and unpredictable.
And the violence of the weather
can call up the violence in the man
so that any moment, like lightning
on the wet streets, he could
put his fist through a window
in a sudden gesture of release
before it's dark again.

WINTER NIGHT UNDER
BLACK MOUNTAIN

A winter sun going down in the west
we drove the other way
out past the leafless vineyards
of the San Joaquin.
Cattle darkened into shadows.
Then it was old loneliness
two solitudes and a long drive
up Auberry Road to the house
under Black Mountain.

On the road we saw the eyes
of animals glitter in the dark.
They were parts of ourselves
we did not yet know
or had known and forgotten.

Now I don't remember
the sound of water
or the smell of the darkness.
All we had was each other
as we walked up the steps
and opened the door
to the house of our absent friends.

When I turned on the porchlight
I saw the oak, arthritic,
the redbud gone to bones
and the white nanny goat
who had come up on the porch
to find shelter from the cold.
I bent over to stroke her neck
and she turned her slow head

to us and I could see then
the bad weather in her eyes
and her body like a mound
of dirty snow.

We covered her with army blankets
offered her water she wouldn't drink
built a windbreak around her
and if we spoke
I don't remember what we said
just our breath blowing away,
white scarves in the wind.

We went in and built a fire
and lay down together
and were lovers. Then you were
asleep beside me in the firelight
your breasts rising and falling.

Tonight with thousands of miles
of weather between us
I think of the odd family
we were. The white goat
lying on the porch, cold
starlight above Black Mountain
where the wind called for her
as it will call for us
and took her away
one breath at a time.

JANUARY

Although the eiders
which I watch daily
rafted together on the harbor
are lovely and I love them
for theirs is the beauty of the world
not human, I won't talk about them
even though they are what enters
my mind when my mind's at rest.
Instead I'll talk about winter
which the eiders, sitting in its lap
in great numbers, so casually endure.
Winter that I, in my twenty-ninth year,
am beginning to understand.
Even my face in the mirror
describes it to me.
Today the snow (which as a boy I never knew)
fell lightly like eiderdown
from the sliced open pillow of the sky.
It smothered the cars and the sound of cars
and the silence of people walking the streets
was equal to the silence of eiders.

A HISTORY

She took him to her bed
and gave him everything:
a child, a home, a history of sighs
and dances. He took out the garbage,
she put up the purple drapes.
He sang and she listened.
She planted rhubarb and tomatoes,
he picked off the worms
and massacred the dandelions.
She lay in the sun, growing more beautiful.
He held her naked against a granite crown,
held her in cold creek water, in owl clover
and lupine, in cars and on the hot sand.
They stood on a cliff above the ocean
and watched the migrations of whales
and shiftings of wind.

They went home
to their fenced yard,
the humming refrigerator
the sweet potato in a glass jar
fading on the sill.
She stared at the television
at the peach tree in the rain.
He listened to the sirens
and would not sleep.
She dreamed of a great white bird.
He marched in a black armband
and imagined the world
reduced to the size of a heart.

She worked days
and heard many voices,
each with its demand.

He drank by a lake in moonlight
and counted his sins.
She lay in bed all day
and soured her pillow with tears.
He came in at dawn
with wet shoes, burrs
in his socks.
She searched him with her silence.
He wanted to show her
what he saw in the air.
He punched out a window.
She kneaded her thighs
and looked deep into the mirror.
Someone else looked back. A face
blurring with the night.
The house burned down,
he offered her the ashes.
The child watched and listened.

§

There is a woman standing in line
in a bank in Modesto.
There is a child walking after rain,
kicking through puddles
ruining the moon that stares
up from the sidewalk.
In the Sierras there is a meadow
of blue camas and a man
bending over the still-warm imprint
where a deer had been resting.

DOWN THE ROAD TO CANYON DAY

Tonight the carcass
of a huge dead dog
lies beside State Highway 73
just a hundred yards north
of the turnoff to Ft. Apache.
All spring and summer
it will lie there. No one
will bury it. No one needs to.
Headlights sweep over the carcass
and light up the big white teeth
and the jaws opened
around a shaft of dark
the headlights can't touch
that starts in the mouth
and goes back through the skull
into the mountains.

When the sun rises
and first light shimmers
in the leaves of cottonwoods
and jewels up
on the surface of the river
and slides off the roofs
of houses and flashes
on the bumpers of pickup trucks
and shines on the slick black
feathers of the raven
picking at the carcass,
that shaft of dark
will still be there
rushing back through bone

into the earth. No one will notice
except a few children
who will carry it away
with them into dreams
down the road to Canyon Day,
Cedar Creek, and Carrizo.

HORSES ON THE HIGHWAY

The road, shining under the headlights,
stretched out behind us.
The ocean two hours to the west.
The farms asleep—fence posts
and barbed wire, a ghostly coyote
hung by the heels as a warning,
steam from the nostrils of cattle,
the fragrance of almond blossoms
and mud.
I held my arm out the window
and felt the cold rain break
on my skin, my palm arched
and jerked like a wing
on the air. Thunder.
The flashed image of orchard, barn,
and silhouette of mountains
in the distance. Joy in just going.
My breath charged with the confusion
of the storm, I sang
whatever the radio sang.

There was no way to know
that a man, careless on a rainy evening,
had left his corral gate open
and five horses, spooked by lightning
or exalted in the rain, were running free
down Highway 41 toward the ocean
or some dreamed field of alfalfa.

In that moment when our lights
touched the splashing tails and big
muscled rumps of horses
the radio went on with its song,
but I hushed
as the hoof came through the windshield
in a spray of glass.
The sound of horse and fender collapsing
was a soft sound
like a hay bale falling from a truck.

Blind for awhile, stunned,
I lay by the horse
and felt the slow beat of rain
as though some great calm heart
had taken over.

IV

THE CIRCLE OF THE YEAR

The circle of the year
closes slowly in the head
or opens
suddenly in the heart.
As once after a night
and a day on the droning Interstate
I looked up
just outside Zanesville, Ohio
and saw a little girl
standing on an overpass
waving at the traffic on I70.
That small hand
stirring the air above Ohio
and the lips moving
where are you going
Hello California, Indiana, Illinois
good-bye good-bye

THE PORPOISE

Today in the middle of Missouri
the temperature dropped forty
degrees in two hours.

Between St. Louis and Kansas City
the traffic was steady.
A banner of black smoke trailed

south from the power plant stack,
mercury slid down in glass.
By dusk the trees were swimming

in the wind. Rain
muted the sound of engines
and made the tires sing.

Then it was nickels and dimes
falling on the roof of the Blue Note
and the Pow-Wow Lounge.

Night came down wherever
it could, fused with the river,
fastened to the windows,

stood up and stretched
in the stunted fields of corn.
South of this darkness

a woman holds the lost warmth
on her skin. Her steady breathing
adding one more degree

to the quiet air around her
as she sits with a book in her lap
and stares out through the screen door

at some memory swimming
in the trees, a porpoise appearing
and disappearing in the Gulf.

And although the dishes need doing
and there's work in the morning
she's composing an idea of beauty—

the skin of the porpoise shines
with the light of two worlds,
this one and this one.

THE NIGHT: GULF SHORES

for Marnie

We sat in the smoke and music
of a bar in Florida.
Let's get out of here you said.
We walked out across the parking lot
to the car in Alabama.
You said you wanted to be big,
as big as the night
that domed the Gulf,
to walk out on the sand
and feel the soles of your feet
press down on the tiny facets
of starlight, to listen
to the murmur of the waves
and the intervals of silence
when some voice of longing
called out of the distance
might find its answer in you
as wind finds its lost body
in the swaying seagrass.

What you find is yours.
Believe it, as so much
needs to be believed.
You are big
even as I watch your small figure
slipping out of sight over the dunes.

Once at evening in the wind
I sat under clatter of palm fronds,
a child, in a dream as vague
as the tide of night rising.

A woman walked toward me
out of shadows
a flower print dress
blowing against her.
She didn't say anything.
She picked me up in her arms
and carried me out into the dark.

TO SLEEP

At night
when the bulldozers are silent
and the earth
begins to give off
the stored up heat of the day
coyotes come down
among the houses.
I lie in bed and listen.
I can feel the houses
huddled together inside me,
and when the coyotes start howling
I let their sound out
slowly with my breath
as I exhale and begin
to drift under the cool stars.

Now the howling is mine.
It's true.
What the houses are saying
is true also.
I hear it everywhere in the night,
an aimless contagion of desire.
Now I am a river
entering the ocean of night.
From here I can go anywhere.
And although the night
is moonless, dark
I can still see clouds forming
and breaking up like crowds
of the lost that traffic in my cells.

They are still hungry.
They still want love.
Their need is a boulder
at the bottom of the ocean.
When I get there
I will embrace it
with my arms of water.

THIS HOUSE

In February I watched gray whales
cruising offshore, just beyond the rocks
and sun-dazzled houses of Laguna.
Though I've closed my eyes
and breathed with them and followed
them down past the slow
blowing curtains of kelp
they won't swim me to sleep tonight.
It's the eighth of April
and this house is a stalled whale
under snow clouds. I know there's
a full moon over Missouri tonight
but the light on your shoulders
is from the parking lot next door.
No sound now but a distant siren
and your steady breathing.
It sets the house adrift.
A few minutes ago I heard a car
pull in and the engine stop.
I waited for the sound of the door,
but whoever it is must still
be sitting in the car.
Someone alone, not wanting to go in,
or maybe lovers at it at last,
what the long evening led up to.
He kisses her neck, her lips,
and moves his hand carefully
to her breast. Her hand rests
its small fire on his thigh.
Their breath freezes on the windows
as the snow begins. .

And as they go down into the current
of their separate hours
I want to imagine something else,
the rolling waves, the moonlight
on the surface of these clouds.
I'll try again. I'll close my eyes,
dream the deep breath and the big heart
so that this house, with you in it,
may rise.

DOLOROSA, ST. CECILIA,
AND THE NIGHT

Somewhere a tiny Sanctus bell
is ringing in a mud church.
To the woman falling asleep
under her black shawl
it is the glitter of a lost instant
in some other life.

Alone in Ensenada
a boy stands up drunk
in the dark of a small room
wanting a woman
staring at the lights
on the water of Bahia Todos Santos.

All the saints of the water
rise with him in the dark
to the street music of mariachis
to the moaning of cattle on the docks
and soft rumbling of ships
ready to sail before dawn
where men smoke
and women burn in the rising
and falling of the coals,
or bathe in small phosphorescent waves
that follow each other to shore,
and the woman who steps from the waves
with the glitter of the sea
in her hair turns

and leaves him standing there
staring out the window
at a path of emerald light
laid across the bay

that a boy might row or swim
all the way
to Punta Banda, or further,
to some other life.

§

She had driven down the dirt road
to the Mission San Xavier del Bac.
Now she sits alone inside the church.
A blue-eyed wooden saint
stares at the painted ceiling of heaven
where the moon is broken.
His blue satin robe is hung
with *milagritos*, a little silver arm,
a leg, a heart, and plastic wristbands,
those worn by hospital patients,
and snapshots of children and soldiers,
mementos of all those who needed a prayer
pinned there, close, so the saint
would not forget them.

This woman who needed a prayer
who in another life
may have been Dolorosa
sits in silence under the vaulted
adobe dome among the saints
and painted angels. She sees
that what life they have, and it is clear
a spirit clings to them, came
from the forests of the Pyrenees,
the Sierra Madre, from the trees
that gave the wood
from which they were carved
with great care.

73

The chipped and faded paint
gives off a light like a stillness
in the eyes of the painter.
Odor of salt and skin
has seeped into the walls
and garments of the saints
from hundreds of years of human use.
Even the fixed eyes of the angel Gabriel
are softened a little
from staring so long in candlelight
from having been looked into
by so many pleading eyes.

She doesn't pray but instead dreams
a few clear notes
from the black bells that hang
in the tower, and she drifts
with the ghosts in that music

back to an orchard of fig trees
and a farm worker's shack
shaded by the gray limbs of olives
where the twilight settled
like gauze in the treetops
and a few stars burned faintly
each night with the knowledge
of distance.

Knowledge and distance
pushed into her as the trees
groaned and the earth hardened

until she came apart
in the eyes of people she loved
and each landscape
that had lived in her
and nourished her living
took back what it had given.

But here in this old room
built where the waters gather
she can remember now a night
that opened above her
and the water in the trough
where she lay on the bottom
and held her breath
and looked straight up at the broken moon,
scattered pieces of light
that formed again, when she held still,
a full moon wobbling on the surface
above her.

§

In another life
I might have been a wood-carver
paying out the hours fashioning
the countenance of a saint,
but in this one, tonight
I am driving alone
down a desert road under the half moon
just outside of Tucson.
The radio is tuned to a station
in Mexico. A woman is singing
Dolorosa O Dolorosa . . .

When the car ahead of me slows
and turns off on the mission road
I follow slowly in its dust
past the shapes of saguaro and mesquite
past the white crosses of the *camposanto*
where the moonlight reminds
of losses and losses to come.

I pull up in front of the mission,
turn off the engine, step outside
and stand here, as the dust settles
and the night grows large around me.
There's a dog barking somewhere south,
and up among the stars
the blinking red light of a jet heading west.

I come here to listen to the music,
the music of the soul of this place
given to it by all the others
who came here for their own reasons.

Before I go in
I'll stand here in the night awhile
and hum a little tune
to the headless statue of St. Cecilia
who clutches a stone tambourine
and pays me the same attention
she does the wind, or the surf sound
of trucks a mile off on the Interstate,
or the white walls of the mission
that seem to hum too
in this moonlight that holds them in place.

§

Once I came here
after a week of fever.
Christmas Eve, and the midnight mass
an hour away.
The white domes of the mission shone
under drifting clouds
silvered by the moon.
I walked in and sat down
and admired the ancient walls
and carved wooden *santos*
and the candlelight.
There were two silver-haired
white ladies sitting side by side
in the last row
and no one else but me and the spirits
until the old doors opened
and a man walked in, a Papago
wearing a trench coat and holding
a straw hat in his hands.

Then came a drunken long-haired man
with some moonlight still in his eyes.
He spoke loudly in Papago to the first man
then rocked like a barrel
up the aisle to the main altar
where he stood and crossed himself
and looked up at the statue
of St. Francis Xavier who looked up at God.

It was quiet again for a moment
then the drunken man began to pray
in earnest, complaining, beseeching,

waving his arms and clenching his fists
until he tired and knelt down.
By now a woman and a small boy
stood beside him at the altar.

She lifted the boy so that he
could kiss the garment of the saint.
Then she placed her hand
on the shoulder of the man
whose prayer had turned to sobbing.
She joined him in sympathy
and before long the boy was crying too.

Now a little man came in
dressed in jeans with cuffs rolled up
and a red flannel shirt.
His prayer, which began at the altar
and which he took to each of the saints,
was a dance, his dark hands tracing
in the air, his head and one shoulder
after the other bowing, knees bending
and his mouth moving rapidly,
soundlessly in devout speech.
He looked each of the saints in the eye,
he looked at the ceiling and gestured,
he looked at the floor and bowed.
Then he joined the woman, the child,
and the weeping drunk man
huddled around the sepulcher
and together they pinned a dollar
on the blue satin garment of the saint.

§

But tonight
is not a night for pilgrims
or for prayer. There's something
in the music, the hum of water
in the roots of the ocotillo
that lays its shadow arms on my shoulders,
and a breeze from the Sea of Cortez
that has swept down the dirt roads
of Sonora and entered the open windows
and carried off the breath
of sleepers in Hermosillo
and swirled in the small ear
of the virgin of Magdalena
and moaned in the empty shells
of the great sea turtles of Desemboque
and dispersed the smoke of Nogales
and broken over the windshields of trucks
and quivered the flanks of the horses
of Sonoita

and then it comes to me
and stops like someone telling a story,
getting the details right
and I hold it a moment in my breath
and know what it is worth
and let it go and hear it turn
in the forged iron bells of Bac
and then move off through the dry grass,
some lover departing as air.

WHO WAS ANTONIO AZUL?

Once I asked the children
of Casa Grande, or Cassa Grand,
depending on who you are, to tell me
their oldest memories and their dreams.
There was a boy in the first row
whose eyes grew wide and thoughtful.
His name was Enis, and he said
he remembered the rain on the roof
of the building where he was born.
He closed his eyes and made the sound
so we could all hear.

Then, Blanca Rios, a thin girl
in the back row raised her hand
and told us the time
in her grandmother's house
when the wind moaned like an old woman
and the night scratched at the window
above her bed and when she looked up
she saw the blood on the nails
of *La Mano Peluda*, the hairy hand.

Another time
in the school at Casa Blanca,
or Cassa Blanka, depending,
I walked in and stared
at the staring faces of the Pima children.
I wasn't sure what to say
so I asked them
Who was Antonio Azul?

And when no one answered
I thought of the long awkward hour
we would share. Then I asked them
again and quickly answered—
Who was Antonio Azul?
I was. I could have been
a sparrow or a snake
but I was Antonio Azul
if only for a little while.
Like my father I was chief
of the Pimas, the river people
of the Gila. My friends called me
Spread Leg because of the way I walked,
or Lion Shield or by other names
less elegant. My father, Culo, was
also called Urine . . .
and by now the children
were laughing and urging me on,
"Say more, Antonio, say more!"

PITT POETRY SERIES
Ed Ochester, General Editor

Dannie Abse, *Collected Poems*

Claribel Alegría, *Flowers from the Volcano*

Jack Anderson, *Toward the Liberation of the Left Hand*

Jon Anderson, *In Sepia*

Jon Anderson, *Looking for Jonathan*

John Balaban, *After Our War*

Michael Benedikt, *The Badminton at Great Barrington; Or, Gustave Mahler & the Chattanooga Choo-Choo*

Michael Burkard, *Ruby for Grief*

Kathy Callaway, *Heart of the Garfish*

Lorna Dee Cervantes, *Emplumada*

Robert Coles, *A Festering Sweetness: Poems of American People*

Leo Connellan, *First Selected Poems*

Fazıl Hüsnü Dağlarca, *Selected Poems*

Kate Daniels, *The White Wave*

Norman Dubie, *Alehouse Sonnets*

Stuart Dybek, *Brass Knuckles*

Odysseus Elytis, *The Axion Esti*

John Engels, *Blood Mountain*

John Engels, *Signals from the Safety Coffin*

Brendan Galvin, *The Minutes No One Owns*

Brendan Galvin, *No Time for Good Reasons*

Gary Gildner, *Blue Like the Heavens: New & Selected Poems*

Gary Gildner, *Digging for Indians*

Gary Gildner, *First Practice*

Gary Gildner, *Nails*

Gary Gildner, *The Runner*

Bruce Guernsey, *January Thaw*

Mark Halperin, *Backroads*

Patricia Hampl, *Woman Before an Aquarium*

Michael S. Harper, *Song: I Want a Witness*

John Hart, *The Climbers*

Samuel Hazo, *Blood Rights*

Samuel Hazo, *Once for the Last Bandit: New and Previous Poems*

Samuel Hazo, *Quartered*

Gwen Head, *Special Effects*

Gwen Head, *The Ten Thousandth Night*

Milne Holton and Graham W. Reid, eds., *Reading the Ashes: An Anthology of the Poetry of Modern Macedonia*

Milne Holton and Paul Vangelisti, eds., *The New Polish Poetry: A Bilingual Collection*

David Huddle, *Paper Boy*
Lawrence Joseph, *Shouting at No One*
Shirley Kaufman, *The Floor Keeps Turning*
Shirley Kaufman, *From One Life to Another*
Shirley Kaufman, *Gold Country*
Ted Kooser, *Sure Signs: New and Selected Poems*
Larry Levis, *Wrecking Crew*
Robert Louthan, *Living in Code*
Tom Lowenstein, tr., *Eskimo Poems from Canada and Greenland*
Archibald MacLeish, *The Great American Fourth of July Parade*
Peter Meinke, *Trying to Surprise God*
Judith Minty, *In the Presence of Mothers*
James Moore, *The New Body*
Carol Muske, *Camouflage*
Leonard Nathan, *Dear Blood*
Leonard Nathan, *Holding Patterns*
Kathleen Norris, *The Middle of the World*
Sharon Olds, *Satan Says*
Greg Pape, *Black Branches*
Greg Pape, *Border Crossings*
Thomas Rabbitt, *Exile*
James Reiss, *Express*
Ed Roberson, *Etai-Eken*
Eugene Ruggles, *The Lifeguard in the Snow*
Dennis Scott, *Uncle Time*
Herbert Scott, *Groceries*
Richard Shelton, *Of All the Dirty Words*
Richard Shelton, *Selected Poems, 1969-1981*
Richard Shelton, *You Can't Have Everything*
Gary Soto, *The Elements of San Joaquin*
Gary Soto, *The Tale of Sunlight*
Gary Soto, *Where Sparrows Work Hard*
David Steingass, *American Handbook*
Tomas Tranströmer, *Windows & Stones: Selected Poems*
Alberta T. Turner, *Lid and Spoon*
Chase Twichell, *Northern Spy*
Constance Urdang, *The Lone Woman and Others*
Constance Urdang, *Only the World*
Ronald Wallace, *Tunes for Bears to Dance To*
Cary Waterman, *The Salamander Migration and Other Poems*
Bruce Weigl, *A Romance*
David P. Young, *The Names of a Hare in English*
Paul Zimmer, *Family Reunion: Selected and New Poems*